With the new day comes
new strength and new thoughts.

—Eleanor Roosevelt

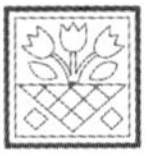

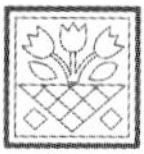

> Every day is a new beginning.
> Treat it that way. Stay away from what might
> have been, and look at what can be.
>
> —MARSHA PETRIE SUE

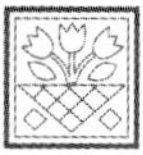

Keep your face always toward the sunshine—and shadows will fall behind you.

—Walt Whitman

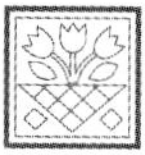

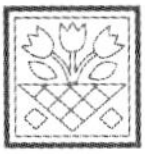

I hope you realize that every day is a fresh start for you. That every sunrise is a new chapter in your life waiting to be written.

—Juansen Dizon,
Confessions of a Wallflower

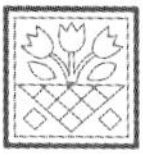

Each day provides its own gifts.

—Marcus Aurelius

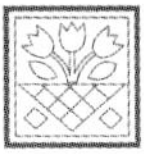

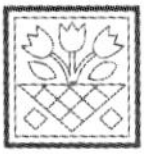

The next morning dawned bright and sweet, like ribbon candy.

—Sarah Addison Allen,
Garden Spells

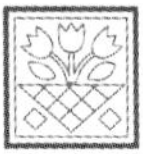

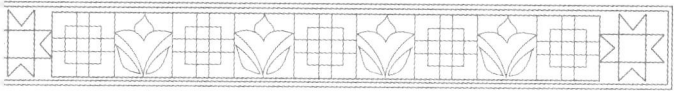

With this morning's sunrise comes a day of things that have never been.

—Toni Sorenson

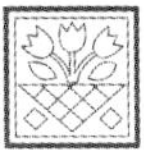

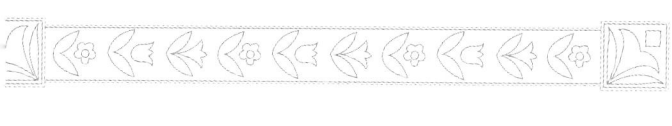

arise full of eagerness and energy, knowing well what achievement lies ahead of me.

—Zane Grey

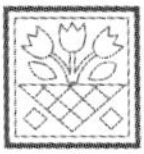

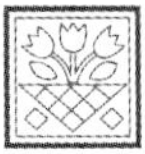